I0815396

ONCE UPON A KWANZAA

Written by **NYASHA WILLIAMS** and **SIDNEY ROSE McCALL**

Illustrated by **SAWYER CLOUD**

RP|KIDS
PHILADELPHIA

Once upon a Kwanzaa, around the world, nestled in homes,
gathered families made up of many shapes, tastes, sizes, and tones.

KWANZAA
DONATIONS

Every space and place had to be just right
to make room for the Nguzo Saba—
the seven principles that make up the history
and foundation of Kwanzaa!

UMOJA (unity)

KUJICHAGULIA (self-determination)

UJIMA (collective work and responsibility)

UJAMAA (cooperative economics)

NIA (purpose)

KUUMBA (creativity)

IMANI (faith)

Many roots and routes to Kwanzaa were woven,
planted, and sung out across the Black Earth.

From the Black neighborhoods and towns, across mountains
and seas, to Los Angeles, the city of the holiday's birth.

While this world holds the memories of the Middle Passage shaped by water, slavery, rebellions, land, and civil rights, our roots run deep in a history colored by miracles, magic, and lights.

Before the candles are lit, the children make space for the mkeka, made of woven raffia, paper, or colored thread.

While the grown-ups bring out food and flowers,
the Elders fill up the kikombe cha umoja,
from which everyone will sip before breaking bread.

The youngest passes out the muhindi to all the children
to honor new growth and community over generations.

As the drums beat and water songs begin, the Elders speak
and pour a libation for the diasporas across populations.

LIBATION STATEMENT

For The Motherland cradle of civilization.

For the ancestors and their indomitable spirit.

For the Elders from whom we can learn much.

For our youth who represent the promise for tomorrow.

For our people, the original people.

For our struggle and in remembrance
of those who have struggled on our behalf.

For Umoja, the principle of unity
which should guide us in all that we do.

For the creator who provides
all things great and small.

Everyone all around has labored with love to craft their zawadi, each handmade and homespun.

The kinara is front and center, candles held and lined up—
seven, six, five, four, three, two, one.

Habari gani? Umoja (Unity)

The first night of Kwanzaa is Umoja, which celebrates building bridges between family, friends, and community.

Our family honors and shares the labors of love from our garden with our neighbors, embracing the principle of unity.

Habari gani? Kujichagulia (Self-Determination)

The second night of Kwanzaa is about naming, reclaiming, creating, reimagining, and living freely.

We use our collective voices in song to lift, support, and give space for us to grow and explore unapologetically.

Habari gani? Ujima (Collective Work and Responsibility)

The third night of Kwanzaa is about understanding the power of working together and building strong teams.

Whether on the field, in the classroom, at the table, or onstage, our neighborhood breathes life into seemingly impossible dreams.

Habari gani? Ujamaa (Cooperative Economics)

The fourth night of Kwanzaa is about using our histories, memories, and recipes as tools to reimagine future wealth.

By finding ease in our local spaces and places, we make room for sharing resources toward abundance and communal health.

BOOKS
LLECTIVE LIBERATION

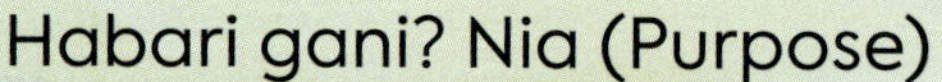

Habari gani? Nia (Purpose)

The fifth night of Kwanzaa is about remembering who we are
as individuals of a global community full of different and diverse hues.

Our family honors this principle by reclaiming time and space
for the water of our soul's callings, wading in purples and blues.

Habari gani? Kuumba (Creativity)

The sixth night of Kwanzaa is about creating roots and routes that nurture the planet and people of tomorrow.

We awaken miracles and magic through our art, allowing joy and justice to overflow.

Habari gani? Imani (Faith)

The last night of Kwanzaa is about finding a place in our everyday lives for hope toward all that can be.

Each day we will learn, dream, organize, and grow together until we are all free.

Our roots in the soil and soul of Mother Africa
reach far and wide.

Kwanzaa is an ancestral commitment toward daily actions that extend beyond any holiday.

As you continue to grow your community, use the seven principles to guide you along the way.

Harambee! Harambee! Harambee!

WORDS TO KNOW

DIASPORA (dai-AS-per-UH): people far from their ancestral homelands

HABARI GANI? (hah-BAHR-ee GAH-nee): Swahili term that asks "What's happening?" or "What is the news?"

HARAMBEE (hah-RAHm-bay): a call of unity cried out at the end of each nightly celebration, meaning "Let's pull together!"

IMANI (ee-MAHN-ee): belief or faith

KARAMU (kah-RAH-moo): the big feast traditionally held on December 31, the sixth day of Kwanzaa

KIKOMBE CHA UMOJA (kee-com-bay chah oo-moe-jah): a wooden cup that represents the unity of family in Kwanzaa celebrations. Take a sip from the cup and then raise it and announce "Harambee." Once you have done this, pass the cup on to the next participant so they may perform the same ritual

KINARA (kee-nah-rah): a candleholder for seven candles used in celebrating Kwanzaa

KUJICHAGULIA (koo-jee-chah-GOO-lee-ah): one of the seven principles of Kwanzaa, the symbol of self-determination

KUUMBA (koo-OOM-bah): the sixth principle of Kwanzaa, this represents creativity

KWANZAA (KWAHN-zah): a celebration of African American culture and heritage, observed by many African Americans from December 26 to January 1

LIBATION (lai-BAY-shuhn): an act of pouring a liquid as an offering

MAZAO (maah-zow): the crops that represent African harvest

MKEKA (em-KAY-kah): a woven mat that represents history and tradition

MUHINDI (moo-heen-dee): the corn that represents our children and the future

NGUZO SABA (n-GU-zo SAH-bah): the seven principles upon which Kwanzaa is based

NIA (NEE-ah): purpose or goal

UJAMAA (oo-jah-MAH-ah): a word that represents family and symbolizes cooperation

UJIMA (oo-JEE-mah): the third principle of Kwanzaa, this symbolizes responsibility and working together

UMOJA (oo-MOE-jah): the Swahili word for unity, this is the first principle of Kwanzaa

ZAWADI (sah-wah-dee): the Swahili term for gift

Pronunciation Tip: Swahili consonants are pronounced like English consonants. The "r" is similar to Spanish and is pronounced by rolling the tongue. Swahili vowels are pronounced as follows: a (ah), e (ay), i (ee), o (oe), u (oo). In most Swahili words, the accent is placed on the next-to-last syllable.

Running Press Kids
Hachette Book Group
1290 Avenue of the Americas, New York, NY 10104
www.runningpresskids.com
@runningpresskids

Distributed in the United Kingdom by Hachette UK Ltd.,
Carmelite House, 50 Victoria Embankment, London, EC4Y 0DZ

First Edition: September 2025

Published by Running Press Kids, an imprint of Hachette Book Group, Inc.
The Running Press Kids name and logo are trademarks of Hachette Book Group, Inc.

The Hachette Speakers Bureau provides a wide range of authors for speaking events.
To find out more, go to www.hachettespeakersbureau.com or email HachetteSpeakers@hbgusa.com.

Running Press books may be purchased in bulk for business, educational, or promotional use.
For more information, please contact your local bookseller or the Hachette Book Group
Special Markets Department at Special.Markets@hbgusa.com.

Print book cover and interior design by Frances J. Soo Ping Chow

Library of Congress Cataloging-in-Publication Data
Names: Williams, Nyasha, author. | McCall, Sidney Rose, author. | Cloud, Sawyer, illustrator.
Title: Once upon a Kwanzaa/written by Nyasha Williams and Sidney Rose McCall;
illustrated by Sawyer Cloud.
Description: First edition. | Philadelphia: Running Press Kids, 2025. | Audience: Ages 4–8. |
Summary: "An engaging picture book celebrating the beautiful traditions of Kwanzaa,
from the author of *I Affirm Me: The ABCs of Inspiration for Black Kids*"—Provided by publisher.
Identifiers: LCCN 2024030947 | ISBN 9780762487356 (hardcover)
Subjects: LCSH: Kwanzaa—Juvenile literature. | African Americans—
Social life and customs—Juvenile literature.
Classification: LCC GT4403.W574 2024 | DDC 394.2912—dc23/eng/20241009
LC record available at https://lccn.loc.gov/2024030947

ISBN: 978-0-7624-8735-6

Printed in Dongguan, China

APS, 05/25

10 9 8 7 6 5 4 3 2 1